CLIMB!

A BOOK OF HOPE, STRENGTH, AND JOY

MARK D. SANDERS & TIA SILLERS

RUTLEDGE HILL PRESS™ NASHVILLE, TENNESSEE
A DIVISION OF THOMAS NELSON, INC. WWW.THOMASNELSON.COM

For ZOE MAGGIPINTO, and all the dear friends we've lost among the mountains. We envy you your heavenly view. And we miss you, always.

DESIGN BY JACKSON DESIGN: DESIGN AND ART DIRECTION BY BUDDY JACKSON AND LINDA BOURDEAUX, NASHVILLE, TN; WWW.BJACKSONDESIGN.COM.

PUBLISHED BY RUTLEDGE HILL PRESS, A DIVISION OF THOMAS NELSON, INC., P.O. BOX 141000, NASHVILLE, TENNESSEE 37214.

ISBN 1-4016-0078-6

PRINTED IN THE UNITED STATES OF AMERICA
03 04 05 06 07 08 — 5 4 3 2 1

CLIMB!

Three years ago we wrote a song and a little book, both called "I HOPE YOU DANCE," and, to put it simply, it changed our lives. Suddenly, we had strangers coming up to us saying things like "I'm so amazed you found a way to put into words all the things I've never been able to say to the people I've loved the most." Or, "We carved your words on my mother's tombstone; used your words in our graduation ceremony; listened to your words on *Oprah*." And invariably, after they've poured their hearts out, they get a little misty-eyed, and we can tell they must be thinking, *these two – this man and this woman – they've got it all figured out.*

WRONG. The only thing we've really mastered is how to say "Thank you!" For three years now we've been speechless. We've smiled and nodded a lot. We've tried not to let on that we're still pretty mystified about this skin we're in. And we don't want anybody to think we're frauds, God forbid.

That's WHY we wrote this book. Because neither one of us – neither Tia nor Mark – has it all figured out. We struggle with faith, with commitment, with depression, with guilt, with weaknesses, with life.

Alcoholics Anonymous speaks of a program of progress and not perfection. The Bible says to let the person without sin cast the first stone. Books about abuse speak of growth through turmoil. Throughout history all sorts of people have advanced all sorts of theories about this human struggle. And so far, only the insane have purported to have all the answers. WE DON'T HAVE ALL THE ANSWERS. Does that mean we're sane?

WE DO KNOW ONE THING FOR SURE:

Nobody ever figures it all out.

But that doesn't mean you shouldn't try. What would you be if you didn't try? It's only out of questioning and searching that there comes a sense of awareness, a moment of peace, a glimpse of serenity. It's empowering to try to simplify this mysterious life, to put into words all the thoughts and feelings that can seem so impossible to understand. And that's what we've tried to do with this book.

We've distilled the art of living down to some active verbs: *Think, talk, listen, discuss, emote, pray, try, hope, love, learn, reach,* and, above all:

climb!

So come along now. We're ready to introduce you to our favorite metaphor for life's challenges: MOUNTAINS. Come learn what you'll need – what we all need – to get over these mountains. Come see what's better left behind. Come see what these mountains are made of. Come climb.

P.S. Right now there are three of us: You and Tia and Mark. When you turn this page, Tia and Mark will, as if by magic, dissolve, merge, and meld into one voice. From here on in it's just the two of us: You, Compadre, and Me.

—⁂—

When I was fourteen my dad's alcoholism had gotten completely out of control. He would come home drunk or not come home at all. We were about to be evicted from our apartment; my mom was working nights, trying to keep us together by day, trying to make sense of what nobody seemed to want to talk about. Finally it got to be too much for all of us. My family split up, each of us going to live with some other family. I spent what was left of my senior year waking up in a strange bed, wondering where my dad was, if he was still alive, wishing we were still together. I was lost, completely. That's a mountain. We didn't know it at the time – my mom and brother and sisters and I – but we were climbing. This book would have helped me back then. I hope it helps you.

—⁂—

KINDS
OF MOUNTAINS

1

Work with me here. There are two kinds of mountains, and this book is about only one of them. Have I got you mixed up? Befuddled? Good.

Life can be befuddling.

THINK OF IT THIS WAY: The first kind of mountain, the kind that this book isn't about, is a thing you can see and touch, like the Rockies and the Appalachians; it's the kind you drive over, the majestic stone towers you snap photos of on summer vacation, or ski down in the winter. You climb those mountains by choice, for fun and adventure. Of course there are even bigger, more ominous, forbidding, and still very real mountains, like the Himalayas, that you see pictures of in *National Geographic* at your dentist's office. Some folks climb those mountains because "they are there" (or so the severely frostbitten lone survivor says to the shivering throng of reporters from the Everest base camp at fourteen thousand feet, minutes before he's life-flighted back to civilization. And nine months before his much-ballyhooed-soon-to-be-made-into-a-TV-movie-book comes out).

This kind of mountain belongs to the earth. It's made of shale and granite, of limestone and ice.

THEN THERE'S THE OTHER KIND OF MOUNTAIN. You won't find its kind on a map because no topographer can chart it. You won't find it in a book or magazine because it can't be caught on film. These mountains pop up out of nowhere. They erupt right there in the middle of your recently paved scenic highway of life – without warning. They aren't the sort that you spy in the distance, that you prepare for in advance, that you pick a nice clear day to tackle. These mountains are not the kind you brag about conquering around the watercooler or capture in some picture on your mantel.

This kind of mountain belongs to us, humanity. It's made of adversity and ordeal, of heartache and hard knocks.

This other kind, these mountains of life, that's our kind of mountain. Our mountains are far more demanding because they don't give you a choice. They don't wait for you to have a weekend free. When they want you, they get you. And they can break you clean in two, leave you bitter, paralyzed, scared to death, before you even figure out which way is up. And sometimes you're the only one who even knows they're there. And the only reason you know they're there is because you're furiously climbing for all you're worth. ALL BY YOURSELF...

No ropes, no oxygen, no subzero parka. NO REPORTER WAITING TO HEAR YOUR STORY OF SURVIVAL.

surv

If you're reading these words, it means you've survived this far, be it by the proverbial skin of your teeth, or maybe even with what they call "flying colors." It doesn't matter. You're here, breathing, heart still beating, maybe worn out from all the walking, but still walking. Maybe tired from all the climbing, but still climbing. You're one of countless survivors.

SURVIVORS...

STILL ALIVERS.

And trust me, to be a survivor with heart and soul intact is no small accomplishment! To be a survivor who is courageous enough to keep seeking and hoping in spite of the obstacles is, in a word, beautiful. Please realize that. Let yourself be proud of the fact that you're here and thriving!

Yes, you're here. And if you're going to be here, YOU MIGHT AS WELL BE HERE WITH SOME PANACHE (however you say that word), some zing, some zip, some zeal. Put a rose between your teeth, a daisy behind your ear. Pin a medal on your chest. Give yourself a box of chocolates. Practice your tango, perfect your fox trot. In the day in and day out of life, you're bound to meet some mountains.

And if you're going to climb these mountains – and I know you are – you might as well be prepared to do a little dance when you get to the top. Believe it or not, these mountains actually make excellent dance partners, once the music starts. And besides, if you were a mountain, which would you prefer: TO BE WALKED ON OR DANCED WITH?

Shall we learn to dance?

My best friend was murdered in Berkeley, California, when he and I were both twenty-two years old. When you're that age, with the world as your oyster, you feel immortal, untouchable. Death is an impossibility, something that only happens to other people. Until the day that someone took his life, I didn't realize how very fragile we are. The hole in my heart was enormous.

That's a mountain.

I was ill-prepared to handle my life at that point (who would be?). I leaned on a couple of close friends and family, somehow making it through each day, figuring maybe somewhere along the way I'd get over it. It took a good twenty years.

That's climbing.

THE
CHOICES

(2)

LET'S SURVEY THE HORIZON, TAKE A LOOK AT THE FUTURE, the peaks ahead of you, of me, of some of us, of all of us:

- Mt. K-12-College
- Mt. Failed Algebra (twice)
- Mt. I Think Dad Is an Alcoholic
- Mt. My Mom Is Always Sad
- Mt. He Broke Up with Me on the Phone
  (might be just a hill, that one)
- Mt. I Just Lost My Job
- Mt. Left Standing at the Altar
- Mt. I'm Getting Divorced
- Mt. I Need to Lose 87 Pounds
- Mt. The Doctor Says It's Cancer

They're out there waiting for you, tall mountains, big challenges. And every one of them, no matter what their size, can consume you, control you. Depending on the time and place and frame of mind you're in, FAILING ALGEBRA CAN FEEL LIKE THE END OF THE WORLD.

This is where it's helpful to have some perspective. And perspective can be had only through experience. And experience comes from clocking in hours on earth. SO LET'S GET A LITTLE PERSPECTIVE HERE. Let's look back on things we've already learned through experience. There's a mountain out there that every single one of us has already climbed, and climbed rather famously, I might add.

birth

Birth is the first mountain. "Not fair!" you say. "I didn't ask for that mountain, I didn't even know I was climbing it while I was climbing it!" Well that much may be true, but your mother sure knew she was climbing a mountain and I guarantee you, there was a heck of a lot of kicking and screaming going on from the both of you.

1

Cut to the birth canal. You're a mere three minutes away from being born. Your mother's in labor, unable to hold you inside any longer. Can't you just picture yourself thinking, *This is it. This is the end!* And then strange hands catch you and strange sounds fill your ears and strange air is sucked in and a strange voice cries out – your voice. And that first terrified cry out loud sounds an awful lot like... "WHYYYYYY MEEEEEEE?!?"

"Why me?" you ask. Because it's your turn. "Why not," said the bearded psychiatrist (with a slight Germanic accent). You were due. For a change. You were due for a change. So as the air fills your lungs, you do what comes naturally. YOU CRY. YOU WAIL LIKE A HAILSTORM. Your first seconds are a battle of will and nature and biology and you lose (don't take it personally, we all lose that one). Maybe you don't want to change, but life makes you change. Maybe you don't want to breathe, but nature makes you breathe. Maybe you don't want to leave, but baby, it's time to go.

IN THE FIRST LONG MINUTE OF LIVING, you've already learned some big lessons. Lessons you'll keep learning (and keep forgetting, if you're anything like everybody else) for the rest of your life.

- Like you can't always get what you want.
- Like change is scary.
- Like sometimes the things you're the most afraid of aren't so bad after all (more on that later).
- Like once the journey starts it never slows down until that last breath. (And who wants to talk about that right now? Not you. You've just been born.)

In that first long minute of living, you've already climbed your first MOUNTAIN.

THERE'S NOTHING LIKE LOOKING BACK ON THE MIRACLE OF BIRTH to give us all a healthy dose of perspective. Suddenly getting broken up with on the phone or trying to get through tenth grade seems a lot more survivable. Even losing a job or getting stood up at the altar might be a splendid opportunity in disguise. Many of these mountains offer a chance for a "rebirth," a chance for a new and better you. And it's that kind of positive spin, that kind of hope, that gives you the strength and the courage not to be afraid of the mountain range ahead of you.

What are you going to do when the next mountain comes your way?

choice #1: Turn back, tuck tail and run, transfer the angst you're avoiding to your cat, your car, your primal scream therapist. In other words, don't deal with it.

choice #2: Try to find a way around, though that might take forever, and forever is not a notion that fits in between Monday and Friday, between Now and Then, between Birth and Death.

choice #3: Stay put, and spend the rest of your days waiting and wondering and wandering the foothills of "What If?" or "Why Didn't I?"

You could choose any of the above, but you won't. You've invested more in this life than that. You have too much gumption and curiosity and respect for yourself to sell yourself short.

WHEN THERE'S A MOUNTAIN IN FRONT OF YOU, THERE'S
REALLY JUST ONE THING TO DO:

choice #4:

Sing "The hills are alive" if you want to; call Julie Andrews if you have to. But climb. If you find that you're afraid, that's okay. If you feel like laughing or crying, be my guest. Join the rest of us. If you don't think you can go it alone, call somebody. This living can get awfully overwhelming and you won't be the first to need help with a mountain, for goodness' sake.

But climb.

Climb regardless of the dust blowing in your eyes, the heat beating down on the back of your neck, the frost in your boots. Climb regardless of the "Stop's," the "You're not good enough's," the "No's." Climb and tell yourself, "yes." Unequivocally "yes." Saying "yes" is a choice. Standing tall in the face of adversity is a choice. Climbing is a choice. A choice you can make. A CHOICE YOU WILL MAKE.

These mountains are heart-breaking, heart-stopping terrain. They're uncharted territory and you're a stranger in a strange land because you've never lived this part of your life before, never walked this path until now.

In the great big scheme of things, there is nothing new under the sun. But in the little scheme of things, everything is new...to YOU. You never know what's about to happen, what's around the corner. Mt. Trial and Tribulation could be just ahead. Waiting. Waiting to grow at whim, to get worse at the drop of a hat, to go from a molehill to a mountain and back again. You can't control the mountains. That much is out of your hands. But you can keep walking. YOU CAN KEEP CLIMBING.

—⟋⟍—

I don't tell many people about this. I was teaching school in California. I wasn't born with a gift for teaching. My ex and I weren't talking, again. I was depressed; it was Sunday. I drove up to some deserted parking lot with a hose in my car. I took one end of that hose and stuck it in the exhaust pipe and put the other end under the hatchback. And I sat there in my car smelling the exhaust coming in, wondering how much I could stand before the choice was out of my hands. But I couldn't do it, couldn't sit there long enough to take the life I didn't think I could handle. I'm still here; I've lived a whole other wonderful life since then. I'm still climbing.

—⟋⟍—

WHAT
TO CARRY
WITH YOU

(3)

HOPE   LOVE   STRENGTH   TENDERNESS   FAITH

Hold on more than a minute. Before you get too far along the path that leads to the rest of your life, let me offer you a few things to put in your pack. They're like food and water, only more important, and they weigh a lot less. They will keep you alive when you don't have anything or anybody else, when you're patiently (did I say patiently?) waiting for someone to give you a BREATH-SAVING BOOST.

THESE ARE THE ESSENTIALS, the absolutely, positively unequivocal necessities of the heart and soul. With them, you can climb anything. Without them, it's a hard road. They're the things we too often forget until we're half a day down the trail. Go ahead and put them in your pack now, and fearlessly face the mountains ahead.

hope

(say it again) hope

Before we begin our essay on hope, let's hear a word from
our faithful sponsors, HOPE, INC. FOR THE BEST®.

Ladies and gentlemen,

Herein lies some treacherous ground. Read with caution. Have your wits about you! We're about to say THAT word. *Love*. Don't we all want love? Love is all you need, love is all you need, love is all you need. We talk about it in books and songs, on TV shows and in movies. It's everywhere in every thought and every longing and hopefully (yes, hopefully) in every kiss and every touch. We all want love.

And the good folks at Hope, Inc. want you to have love. But you can't have love...without hope. Hope has to come first. Hope gives you the courage to sail your ship. Love fills its sails. Hope lets you imagine. Love brings that image to life. Hope is all about the future, about a brighter day. Hope makes you cross your fingers, pray, talk to strangers, reach out, try to get up, get up, get back up. It's hope that will help your dreams come true. So help hope help you. Hang in there with Hope, Inc. for the Best®.

Thank you, HOPE, INC. for those insightful words
and for inciting this next question:

Why do we take hope for granted? Well, it isn't sexy like love, not dramatic like heartache, and it isn't in the least bit temperamental or loud or insecure. Hope is quietly confident. Consistently positive. Terminally… hopeful. IN OTHER WORDS, HOPE IS "JUST" HOPE.

BUT "JUST" HOPE IS WHAT MANY PEOPLE DON'T HAVE. There are reasons for this. Some people's brains aren't even wired for hope, can't figure out a way to begin to even contemplate a brighter day, can't find the desire or the will to crawl out of the cave called *depression*. For those people, hope is a word in the dictionary that doesn't make much sense. When somebody's not even wired for hope, how can they know that it's hope they're missing?

Here's where I find myself crossing my fingers and hoping that each and every one of those people can find help. And help can be found in so many unexpected places – from within, from a friend, from a book...in a church, in a doctor's office, or on a walk in the park. It doesn't matter where help comes from as long it shows you that hope can be recovered. Discovered. ALL OVER AGAIN.

THERE ARE WAYS TO MOVE BEYOND DEPRESSION. The cycle of inconsolable sadness can be broken. I know this can happen because it's happened to me and to people I love. But sometimes it's only through help that you can find the will to hope. Please don't take that first step up the mountain without it.

And then there are literally millions of good people who are so consumed with that big word *survival* that they don't have the time or the strength for this little word *hope*. We ache for those people who crave fresh water, who crave one bowl of rice, who crave a warm or dry or safe place to lay their head. For those people, hope is a luxury. BEFORE YOU FEED THE SOUL, YOU HAVE TO FEED THE BODY AND THE BRAIN. That's the human in our humanity. And the beauty of our humanity is that those with hope want to help those without it. I have hope. I'm hoping you have hope.

But just because you have hope doesn't mean you can take it for granted. Hope is a gift. Hope allows you to be grateful for that gift. Hope lets you have faith, faith gives you confidence, confidence leads to joy in living and all of that adds up to the ability to love. To be able to love is a very big deal. And you know how love is the thing that gets all the attention, the thing we want most. We need hope; we want love. We want love because it makes us feel needed; we need hope because we love to feel wanted.

It's a beautiful circle.

"HOPE IS THE THING WITH FEATHERS THAT PERCHES ON THE SOUL." Emily Dickinson said that. Things with feathers can fly away at the drop of a tear. So care well for hope. Take lots of it in your backpack. It won't weigh you down or hold you back. It will stand with you at the base of your latest mountain, lift your eyes till you see the top of that mighty rock and show you the path from where you are to where you know you need to be.

hope
(say it again) hope

love

I know I've been a little hard on love, and for that I apologize. It's just that love is so wonderfully easy to love that sometimes we forget other things are important, and hope is one vital something we don't want to forget or diminish.

SO HAVING SAID THAT, I NOW SAY THIS:

Put love in your pack
and your pack will have wings
of its own.

A LITTLE LOVE POEM:

I think love has wings
I've seen them flutter
From the corner of my eye
I think love moves things
Like men and mountains
One stubborn stone at a time
I think love has vision
'Cause it always seems to find
The wisdom in a fool
I only hope
These things I think I know
Are true

But even if I'm right
Even if I'm wrong
I will keep this faith I have
That keeps me holding on
It's a risk just breathing
Let alone needing
Let alone believing in love
And I believe in love
I believe in love

ONLY LOVE CAN SEE that so much of life comes down to hang-gliding on hope and flying on faith. Only love knows that peace can be found through not understanding the questions, not knowing the answers. Only love can take it or leave it alone, can let it be, sleep like a baby.

Unlike us humans, love is content in not having a map to this peculiar world, this world we are only passing through. I think love must have some kind of internal compass, its own sense of direction. Only love goes by feel, hands outstretched, open and ready to reach, touch, grasp, and hold on to what is worth holding. Somehow love knows what's worth holding on to. Somehow love knows what really matters. And that's why ONLY LOVE CAN BREAK YOUR HEART.

It's the people we count on the most, cherish the most, crave the most, who leave the biggest empty space in our souls when they're gone, when they leave, when they pass on. That's because we love them, and by loving them our own meaning becomes more meaningful. Love empowers, enlightens, enables, and invigorates us. It gives us courage and fortitude, makes us kinder to the rest of the world. And even though we might lose love (or just misplace it for a while), what really matters is that we have loved. And if we have loved, we can love again. AND NESTLED THERE IN THAT THOUGHT, WE FIND HOPE.

And here we live, here we love, in this terrible, wonderful, merciless, merciful world. This world of empty mouths and full stomachs, HOPELESS CASES AND MIRACLE CURES, forlorn souls and unbreakable spirits. Why or how or who gets what seems to be the luck of the draw. To where or to whom we are born surely must be by chance. There is no reason for that, there can't be a reason. But all the while, in every corner and country and cranny of this earth people find and feel thrilled and fulfilled by love.

LOVE HAS BOUNDLESS HOPE.

LOVE HAS ENDLESS FAITH.

AND, UNLIKE US, LOVE NEVER DIES.

And it's because love never dies that love can keep us alive. It can keep us hungry. Just the thought of love can keep us motivated, moving on, one day, one step at a time. These mountains we climb, WE CLIMB IN THE HOPE OF LOVE, in the name of love, for the sake of love. And in those times of our lives that we actually get to hold love in our hearts, the journey becomes that much more unforgettable, that much more wondrous.

So whenever you can, carry love with you. And whenever you can't, carry on.

strength

Here's something else you'll want to take with you for those never-ending uphill stretches. It ranks right up there with taking your vitamins and doing twenty push-ups every morning. It's akin to stretching before you start off, akin to tipping your hat to all the people you meet along the way.

strength

Strength is a tricky subject, subject to trickery. We all want and need to be strong, but too many times strength veers off into being just plain old tough. Now don't get me wrong – tough has its time and its place (think boot camp; think beef jerky). But much of the time maybe what we need is a hand to hold, a level head, a dauntless sense of humor. The Strength to Endure Another Hard Day.

THIS TAP DANCE WE CALL THE RHYTHM OF LIFE TAKES RHYTHM. These vibrant shades of gray we call strength take strength. But not too much – that's tough. Go too far down that road called Strength and you'll wind up at the corner of Untouchable-but-Still-Very-Breakable-Armor-Clad-Heart Avenue or Street or Boulevard. Makes no difference. Don't let yourself go there. Strength is about restraint. Strength takes skill, not brute force.

YOU CAN BE STRONG, BUT GENTLE.

YOU CAN BE STRONG, BUT ACHE.

YOU CAN BE STRONG, BUT FEEL.

STRENGTH IS ALL ABOUT FINESSE, all about getting yourself and others through tough (there's that word, right where we need it) situations with grace and dignity.

Of course, grace and dignity are not always graceful and dignified. Sometimes strength makes you bow your head, maybe even put your tail between your legs. Sometimes you have to say, "I'm sorry," "I was wrong," "I don't know the answer," "I need help." To be strong is to admit, to trust, to forgive, and to try to forget. (I fear that forgetting is a mountain of its own. Our brains don't come with erasers.)

AND **cry**

To be strong means you have to know how to cry. It doesn't do anybody any good to be too tough to cry. You can't let pride get in the way of vulnerability because it's only through letting down your guard and opening yourself up that you become and stay real. If you don't let those tears find a way out of you, if you keep stuffing all those emotions inside, one day you may forget how to feel. One day you might implode (think heart attack, clutching the steering wheel on the way home from work; think breakdown in the frozen-food section of the grocery store – "We have a spill in Aisle 3").

Calm down. Take a few deep breaths. Find your way past Aisle 3. You will be all right. But you have to know how to cry. Period.

IT'S EASIER BEING TOUGH THAN BEING STRONG because all tough requires is being unyielding, incorrigible, and stubborn.

And isn't stubborn fun! You get to say things like "This town ain't big enough for the both of us," and "It's my way or the highway." Granted, sometimes life calls for blowing on your gun and walking away into the sunset, but extreme behavior needs to be saved for extreme circumstances. When that kind of attitude becomes your permanent take on the world, your "tough" can turn into someone else's mountain. Heck, your "tough" can turn into a mountain for you too.

And dear old tough stands by your side only until you need help, until you need to be held. Friend, if there's one thing that's for certain in this life, it's that we will all need holding, come some day. And tough will not hold you. Tough can't. It's just not tough's style. Tough might get you over the hills faster. BUT THIS ISN'T A RACE, and you'll miss the view, and you won't make any friends along the way. (And you get by with a little help from your friends.) Besides, each mountain we are made to climb is subtly different, and tough is not subtle. Each step takes feeling and vision, empathy and sympathy, and those are, unfortunately, attributes that tough does not possess. Don't go with tough. Go with strength. Strength will get you over the mountains. (Oh, and take along some tenderness. We can't forget tenderness.)

tenderness

Most people would say the opposite of *strong* is *weak*. Even Webster's dictionary seems to think so. But the kind of strong I'm talking about really needs tenderness as its counterpart. Strong and tender are what you try to be most of the time. Tough and weak are what you have to be sometimes. There will be days when you have to muster up your best one-two punch, float like a butterfly, sting like a bee, and kick some butt. And that's all right. There will be days when you'll feel so used and used up, you'll want to hide from the world, wear flannel pajamas, and stay in bed all day. That's all right too. Just remember, IT'S WHEN WE'RE WEAK THAT WE MOST NEED TENDERNESS.

BELIEVE IT OR NOT, TENDERNESS TAKES

COU

rage

It doesn't matter whether you're the giver or the receiver, tenderness requires vulnerability and it takes courage to be vulnerable. Being the giver of tenderness means you have to take off your armor and turn off your cell phone. You have to open your heart and commiserate. You have to shut up and listen. Admitting that you're in need of tenderness means you have to ask for a shoulder to lean on. You have to beg the favor of sympathy and understanding. You have to let down your guard and be at the mercy of someone you think you can trust with the part of you that hurts.

That's why we need to search out and surround ourselves with other STRONG, HOPEFUL, AND POSITIVE PEOPLE. When we're feeling weak, a person who's strong can empathize, can sympathize with what we're going through. They hold us in our battered moments because they know we would do the same if the tables were turned.

And tables tend to turn. Sooner or later, every last one of us will need a little tenderness.

So let me gently offer a few words on tenderness:

A DEFINITION:

ten′der·ness (tĕn′dər-nĕs) *n.* **1.** Showing compassion and gentleness. **2.** Giving the gifts of understanding, patience and solidarity: "You and me against the world, kid." **3.** Saying and meaning things like, "Don't cry, sugar, but if you have to cry, come let me hold you" and "Shhh, it's all right now, tell me all about it when you're ready. I'm not going anywhere."

SOME SENSITIVE SUGGESTIONS FOR YOUR LISTENING PLEASURE:

try a little tenderness
(THANK YOU, OTIS REDDING)

you can't be tender too much
(THANK YOU, DOAK SNEAD)

tender is the night
(THANK YOU, BUCK OWENS)

leave a tender moment alone
(THANK YOU, BILLY JOEL)

love me tender
(THANK YOU, THANK YOU, ELVIS)

Tenderhearted
Takes us back to
Where we started,
Sing along.
You can't be tender
In this world
Without being
Strong.

AHA, ANOTHER BEAUTIFUL CIRCLE!

faith

Let's say it's a Tuesday. You've got a good night's sleep and a healthy breakfast under your belt. Your backpack's full of hope, your heart's full of love. Your body feels strong and your mind feels light and willing and tender. The sun is out, the air is crisp, the clouds look harmless enough, and the mountain in front of you looks more like a knoll. You're feeling confident, even a little...INVINCIBLE.

SO UP YOU GO. Maybe you whistle at first, maybe you tell yourself, "Hey, this isn't so bad." But pretty soon your breathing becomes labored – the trail is getting more rugged, more vertical. After a while, you're tempted to turn back. You struggle, you sweat. Tuesday morning melts into Tuesday afternoon, and you still can't see the top. Come Tuesday night it begins to rain, and keeps on raining and raining and raining. And when the sky finally clears and the sun finally shines on cold, wet you, that's when you remember...

You're afraid of heights! Don't look down! Grab onto a tree! TACKLE THAT

ver

vertigo…

vertigo…

Now you want to be positive, yes you do!!! After all, the next bend you come to may be the last! (But it isn't.) The next rise on the horizon may be the summit! (But it isn't either.)

Admit it.

You're on the verge of being...hopeless. You thought you packed enough hope, but as the days have dragged on you've run dangerously low. And now you're afraid you'll never get there, afraid you'll never see the breathtaking view from the top. This is where your emergency supply of faith needs to kick in. This is where the soul goes to work at reviving the spirit. You see, faith takes over when all else fails.

When you hope, you have expectations. You really think, in a rational way, that what you desire, what you're trying to attain, is within reach. But when the going gets tough and keeps getting tougher, that rational person inside you starts to doubt the attainability of your hopes. Starts to think maybe the struggle isn't worth it. Starts to whine and whimper. Enter faith! Somehow faith believes without a doubt, without a single question. Somehow, faith doesn't need a shred of proof. IT JUST BELIEVES THAT YOU INDEED CAN DO THIS!

If hope is heart, THEN FAITH IS SOUL. Faith takes your chin in its hand, looks you square in the eye and says, "Walk on, child." And so you do. You walk on. And then one dawn...

In the fine frosty morning, at an hour heretofore unlived, you reach that elusive summit. There are no more rocks to climb. You have arrived. You turn around slowly and soak up all 360 degrees. How do you feel? What do you see? What do you get? Well, along with a sense of accomplishment, of peace, of a job well done, along with the satisfaction of doing what you set out to do, you get a great view of... The Next Mountain.

BECKONING.
CHALLENGING.
CALLING YOUR NAME.

But wait. Don't feel like you need to run up that next mountain yet. (It's not like it's going anywhere.) Dwell on this one for a while. After all, faith got you this far. And faith fully intends to personally see you over all the mountains in the distance. So make yourself some time. Take yourself a break. YOU DESERVE IT.

Lie back with your hands stretched out behind your head. Watch the wind push the clouds across the sky, let yourself believe you're on top of the world – because in a sense you are. Just be for now, for you. (Who cares if that sounds so new agey – it's true.) Then, when you're ready... pick yourself up, dust yourself off, put that pack on, and start climbing down the other side. One foot in front of the other. That's all you can do. This walk never ends, you know. You're always in uncharted territory. There's always another mountain. But that's what makes life thrilling... and you breathless.

There will be days, there will be times when you'll feel like you've climbed so far, when that voice inside you is complaining that it's been uphill for too long, that this journey is way too hard. That despite all your careful planning and packing, maybe you just don't have what it takes. And then, to top off all that doubt, you'll happen to take your eyes off the trail for a moment, look out on the horizon and spy...

THE BIGGEST MOUNTAIN YOU'VE EVER SEEN.

You'll feel a lump build in your throat, your heart stop, your feet freeze. You'll close your eyes, swallow, count to ten, say the serenity prayer, open your eyes and...It will still be there. THE BIGGEST MOUNTAIN YOU'VE EVER SEEN. You'll swallow again, laugh incredulously, shake your head, and think, *There is absolutely no way I can climb that.*

I HOPE, WITH ALL MY MIGHT, THAT YOU WILL ALWAYS HAVE SOMEBODY WHO HAS FAITH ENOUGH TO TELL YOU THAT YOU CAN. Like I'm telling you now.

It's strange how we can memorize the table of elements or a line from Shakespeare, but WE'RE ALL THE TIME FORGETTING HOW WE NEED TO LOVE AND TRUST AND BELIEVE. It's ironic that we have no trouble keeping track of what time our favorite TV show comes on, but we can't seem to impress upon ourselves that we all need some understanding and some tenderness, some compassion. With that in mind, I've come up with a little mnemonic device that helps me remember what I need to carry with me, and maybe it will help you too.

Next time you're staring at a mountain and you find yourself at a total loss about what to do next,

remember this:

hope says,

"I THINK YOU CAN GET OVER THAT MOUNTAIN;
I REALLY THINK YOU CAN."

love says,

"HONEY, WE'LL CLIMB THAT MOUNTAIN TOGETHER."

strength says,

"GET IN SHAPE. GET YOUR PACK READY. WE ARE
GETTING UP AT FIVE A.M. AND WE ARE GOING TO
CLIMB THAT MOUNTAIN – YOU CAN DO IT!"

tenderness says,

"YOU REST A WHILE. YOU'RE WORN OUT.
TOMORROW'S ANOTHER DAY AND YOU
CAN CLIMB THAT MOUNTAIN THEN."

faith says,

"I BELIEVE YOU CAN CLIMB THAT MOUNTAIN."

My first wife and I divorced after ten years of marriage. My daughter was three when her mom decided to move back to Texas. I would drive ten hours to pick up Kathryn, then ten hours home with her. Two weeks later it would be ten more hours back to Dallas, where I'd watch her walk in that front door and watch that door close.

Those next ten hours, on my way back home alone, when there was no little girl coloring in her car seat, when I'd walk into Arby's without Kathryn hanging onto my hand...those were the loneliest times, the emptiest times. I would listen to songs that meant a lot to me over and over and over, and cry some and yell some. And keep driving away from my little girl. That was a mountain, and I was climbing.

WHAT
TO LEAVE
BEHIND

(4)

REGRET   DENIAL   FEAR   ASSORTED OTHER TIDBITS

THERE ARE MOUNTAINS...

Many of life's challenges are actually rewarding, invigorating, life-affirming. It feels wonderful to finally shed those eighty-seven pounds. It feels exciting to graduate from high school or college, to start a new job. It feels freeing to get a clean bill of health or pay off your credit-card debt. Many challenges are like a 10k run – you get to cross the finish line with your arms in the air. Many accomplishments earn an "I'm so proud of you" or a "You did it!"

AND THEN THERE ARE MOUNTAINS.

Unfathomable heartache, like losing someone you love long before their years should be up, is such a powerful blow to the chest that some people never breathe normally again. Some people become defined by what they used to have, by what they lost, by what was stolen from them. Some people never move beyond the moment their world was shattered.

Each and every one of us will experience dark hours and periods of hopelessness. This is a natural reaction to life's cruel blows. And it's during those times that we're especially susceptible to the hypnotic powers of certain emotions that are not – I repeat, not – good for us. Emotions like regret, denial, and fear. When we are in a painful place, these negative emotions seem to ease the hurt, they seem to speak our same disillusioned language. It becomes tempting to stop climbing when we're feeling so weak and bitter. It's tempting to just give up.

Regret and guilt and blame
Denial and fear and shame
All lead our fragile hearts
To a permanent state of…
pain.

But it doesn't have to be that way. Yes, heartache can and will happen. Yes, there are troubles that will come in the wake of broken dreams and shattered promises. But that HEARTACHE ISN'T SUPPOSED TO LAST FOREVER. And you're supposed to pick up your pack and get back on the trail at some point. Sure, you'll be walking wounded for a while, but at least you'll be walking. And while you're living in that fragile state, you have to be aware that those negative emotions, those powerful forces, are still trying to stop you from moving on. Still putting all kinds of doubts in your head. Trying to steal your hope and strength. Trying to drag you down to their level. It's in those times of weakness that you have to be most careful.

regret

For all the joy and beauty in this world, there is more than a chance you will see more than your share of unimagined sorrow. There comes a morning when the sun can't reach you to warm your soul. There comes a morning when you wake to find a mountain so large that you are nearly swallowed up in its shadows. And in that same instant you feel a hollow space in your chest where, only yesterday, your heart used to be. And sometimes despite all your hope and strength and tenderness, you swear you don't know how to live anymore, don't know how to want to live anymore.

Hold on. Just hold on.

SOMETHING HAPPENS TO US WHEN WE LOVE AND RECEIVE LOVE IN RETURN. We forget that nothing on this earth lasts forever. We believe what we have is surely an exception to the rule, surely something so true and rare will never fade away or be taken from us. Only love can bring that kind of confidence – that kind of consistency. And the concept of love is constant, but the people who love are not. It doesn't matter how much we love, or what we might wish for or work for or pray for. On this earth, everything has its beginning, its season, its end.

Of course, you know this to be true. You understand the rules, you've signed off on the terms of the agreement called life. You know some children are not meant to grow old in this world. You know some people can't rise above their demons no matter how hard you try to help them. You know that everyone has to die somehow, someday. You know all of this, but you don't feel it in the pit of your stomach until some painful truth finds its way to your welcome mat. There you are, standing in the doorway, like a war bride holding an unwanted telegram, trying to make sense of some new reality, of some new you that seems to be less than it was.

You don't have to be told. You already know. YOU'LL NEVER BE THE SAME AGAIN.

In the fog of grief that follows, REGRET BECKONS LIKE A CANDLE IN A WINDOW. We are drawn to it. Regret offers a cool kind of comfort. Regret is a compatriot, a fellow sorrower. It's quick to give shelter in your weakest moments. It will put its jacket around your shoulders, make you some tea, make sure nothing interrupts your heartache, your woe. Regret is very protective, peering through the peephole every time somebody knocks, keeping even your friends out. Regret will quietly explain that you're too tired, too fragile for visitors right now.

Regret is a whisperer, a soft talker, an offerer of what seems to be tender words of understanding on long, lonely nights.

regret says,
"YES. YES, YOU SHOULD HAVE CLIMBED THAT MOUNTAIN. YES, YOU COULD HAVE...BUT YOU DIDN'T."

When we lose something, grief is a process we all must go through. But grief is only a chapter, a phase of life. It isn't meant to go on forever. YOU CANNOT WALK WITH GRIEF, because grief is a mountain; a mountain you climb and then, when you are ready, a mountain you leave behind. And if you try to carry grief with you, you might as well be carrying a sack of stones. Carrying all that weight around will only break you down. Break you down slow.

The danger is this: In grief you can reach for faith or you can cling to regret. And the difference is this: With faith you learn to believe in a future; with regret you can believe only in a past. If you choose regret, you spend your days looking over your shoulder. If you choose regret, you spend your nights losing count of ALL THE THINGS YOU WISH YOU COULD HAVE CHANGED.

BUT THE PAST IS NOT YOURS TO CHANGE.
CHANGE ONLY HAPPENS BY MOVING FORWARD.
AND MOVING FORWARD TAKES

faith

Faith lifts you in its arms. Faith carries you over the mountains that no one should have to climb. Faith finds a rhyme and a reason where before there were none. Faith comes to peace with mortality. Faith sees the bigger picture: a pleasing view of earth, a promising view of the heavens. Faith lets you believe that what you've lost is still a part of you. And that you are still a part of what you've lost. Faith makes a fantastic friend. A real soulmate. Faith gives you the willpower to turn your back on regret and run.

CLIMB WITH FAITH. OR, BETTER YET, DANCE WITH FAITH. Dance with faith all the way to the top of your insurmountable mountains.

denial

This is how denial operates. Denial enables you to ignore the truth. Somewhere along some lousy, unbearable, particularly vulnerable part of your journey, when you're desperate for company, denial will fall in step with you. You'll find yourself drawn in by its pleasant conversation. You'll hear yourself offering to share your camp, share your can of beanie-weenies. And then your fire, then your tent, then your sleeping bag.

And then you're sunk.

THAT LITTLE DEVIL

denial says,

"WHAT MOUNTAIN? I DON'T SEE A MOUNTAIN."

Denial lies.

Period. Denial is masterful when it comes to fooling and confusing you because it wants you to have faith. Blind faith. And surely something as wonderful as faith would never hurt you – right? But denial wants you to put your good faith in the wrong things, things that can hurt you in the long run. Denial wants you to pretend everything's just fine, to close your eyes and not deal with your reality. Denial wants you to believe in it, without doubt, to hide behind it, to mistake it for faith and strength and comfort.

DENIAL WILL SAY ANYTHING TO KEEP YOU FROM CHANGING. It will shield you from the truth, while swearing that it's only trying to protect you. Denial will keep you from putting your ear to the ground, putting those binoculars to your eyes to search, really search, the world around you. You'll never hear the rumble, never see the avalanche coming until it's too late. And even then, buried alive, you'll hear denial's saccharine sweet voice say, "Oh, now isn't this cozy. What avalanche?"

What mountain?!?

(Psst! The power of denial should not be underestimated. When you deny some difficult reality, you eliminate any opportunity to find solutions. You can't be contemplating solutions when you're too busy swearing there's not even a problem.)

WHEN WE SEE OTHER PEOPLE LIVING IN DENIAL we want to shake them and tell them to wake up, that they're hurting themselves. We can say that because we're on the outside looking in, where the view is much better, where there are no conflicting emotions, no crippling addictions, no years invested in a dream gone south.

BUT WHEN THE TROUBLE IS OUR OWN, the truth is so much harder to discern. Denial only has to hide from one person to be effective. You can only see your own messy denial through hindsight or insight. No one else can do that for you. It has to be through your own eyes, looking into your own heart. (It doesn't matter how much people want you to change. You have to want it more than anything or anyone else. And denial doesn't want you to change because change is not what denial is about.)

Hind•sight (hīnd′sīt′) *n.* **1.** Looking back on mistakes. **2.** Putting space between then and now, said space to be occupied by a truer truth. **3.** Taking a bullet in the past in order to know you might want to duck in the future. **4.** First you live, then you learn.

In•sight (ĭn′sīt′) *n.* **1.** Unearthing what wants to hide inside you. No secrets, no myths, no illusions. **2.** Discerning the nature of you, flaws and all. **3.** Learning as you live.

Which sight do you want? Denial can deal with hindsight, because you only grow, if you grow, in the aftermath. In the meantime, denial still gets to wreak its havoc upon you. Hindsight is a good thing only insofar as you really learn from your experiences and as YOU LEAVE THE PAIN IN THE PAST where it belongs. There's nothing wrong with looking back on a time, from a safe distance – eyes wide open and coming to some kind of understanding, some kind of peace. Just remember that, if you let it, hindsight likes to wallow, likes to walk in the rain, hand in hand with regret.

Insight, on the other hand, takes some real diligence and awareness, TWO NATURAL ENEMIES OF DENIAL. Think of insight as a security guard for the soul, as a weekly State-of-Your-Life update. It wants to make sure you're putting your faith or your love in something that is truly worthy of your emotions, of your attention. Insight wants to make sure that your love gets loved back. And who doesn't want that? Who wouldn't like to steer clear of denial, let go of regret and grow? Who wouldn't like to figure out if the mountain ahead is even worth their time, even theirs to climb?

Insight walks with hope and strength. It doesn't expect to journey down the prettiest paths with the most breathtaking views. It doesn't mind if the way gets difficult or winding as long as it's stepping in the right direction. Insight will help you turn off that road of lies and lead you down the PATH OF TRUTH. And that may be the very truth that sets you free.

fear

While you're being diligent and while you're being aware,
be aware of fear. Because fear will never set you free.

Fear likes to hide in the far corner of your world, beneath your greatest weaknesses, where it can keep your mind firmly shut. And when your mind is shut, you are in a very dark place. Fear, you see, has a hard time with light, with movement, with sound, with talking. With breathing. Fear is afraid of options. Afraid that it might disappear if someone else shows up, if the phone rings with a friendly voice at the other end, if there's a knock on the door. Fear is high-strung and short-fused. Fear doesn't know how to count from ten backwards, to take deep breaths, to calm down, to think positive thoughts. FEAR WANTS YOU ALL TO ITSELF, wants you to take that phone off the hook, grab a blanket, bundle up and hunker down all day long. And night, and on and on, until your days and nights are gone. And when you finally run out of time, fear will just move on to someone else.

Fear babbles incessantly,

doesn't listen to reason, doesn't want you to hear good news. Fear is a drag, a drag queen, an illusion, a painted smile that says, "Hold me; I need you to hold me." And don't we all love to be needed?

Fear is jealous.

It doesn't let go easily or gracefully. It holds a grudge and reminds you over and over again just who it was you abandoned. Or who abandoned you. Fear doesn't want you to forget and forgive and move on.

Fear wants you to think

you can count on it, that you can't count on anything else. Fear doesn't want you to find out that there are other choices, that there are ways to rise above, over the mountain, and out from under its shadows. Heck, fear even never climbs a mountain. It reads the book, terrified, with a flashlight under the covers, at 4:00 A.M. Then it falls asleep at dawn.

Fear is a wuss.

fear says,
"RUN FOR YOUR LIFE! IT'S A MOUNTAIN!"

But (and there's always a *but*) WE NEED A LITTLE FEAR IN OUR LIVES. It tempers us. What else makes us stay away from things that sting or burn? What else can make us look both ways or think twice? And that's the rub. You need to have fear in order to understand the risks and the dangers lurking in this world. You need to have fear in order for your internal warning system to work in the first place. You need to respect fear. But you can't let it rule you; you can't be a part of its grand scheme. Safe, there in those dark corners, fear would rule the world.

And it's come close. Fear has brought incredibly evil people to staggering power. Fear, like denial and regret, doesn't want you to think you have a way out. It wants you to sell yourself short. It wants you to accept your fate. Fear enables ignorance, and it's ignorance that makes people think they're better than others. It's ignorance that allows people to accept evil without questioning. IT'S IGNORANCE THAT FUELS HATE.

Ig•no•rance (ĭg′nər-əns) *n.* **1.** Lacking in fundamental knowledge and truths. **2.** If you're not the color of my skin, you're not as worthy as I am. **3.** That's what my daddy taught me and so it has to be right. **4.** Not knowing what you should know.

And you cannot let your soul be defined or colored or filled with hate. You cannot let your heart find comfort or power in that dark mode of thinking. Once you cross that line and give in to the mesmerizing sway of hatred, those amazing gifts like strength and insight lose their power, their vision. Hope can't work its wonderful magic on you. TENDERNESS CAN'T REACH YOU TO HEAL AND HOLD.

SOMEHOW FEAR AND HATRED FORM AN INVISIBLE BARRIER around your body. Like steel, like a bullet-proof shield, hate keeps love out. Brilliantly. Masterfully. Hate smothers you in a way that doesn't let beauty or joy or sunlight in. And your soul needs all these awesome things to grow, to breathe, to thrive. To climb.

It's a difficult thing to be pulled out of the darkness and into the light. But it has been done. Hearts of stone have become hearts of gold. Bodies of water have been parted. Insurmountable mountains have been climbed. Lives have been changed.

IT'S WHAT WE CALL

a miracle

IN WHAT WE CALL

your life.

And now, a minor epilogue with a THIS-IS-YOUR-LIFE-AT-STAKE MESSAGE: I don't want to sound repetitive, and I don't want you to think that I think you haven't been paying attention. But some things bear repeating. Some things demand memorizing, internalizing, and impressing on the brain. So here it goes: REGRET makes you look over your shoulder all the time. DENIAL makes you walk around with your eyes closed. And too much FEAR just keeps you in a constant state of paranoia and panic.

And in case you haven't noticed, we're climbing mountains here!

You can't be looking backward and keep moving forward. You can't shut your eyes tight and make your way around a winding, narrow pass. You can't be having a panic attack when you're only three inches away FROM A FIVE-HUNDRED-FOOT CLIFF!

You are a mountain climber! Look at all you've done! Look at how far you've come! You don't have time to be dallying with regret, denial, or fear. If they're with you right now, you've got to shake them, you've got to leave them behind.

AND GET BUSY MOVING ON.

My mom picked a bad time to decide to die. She was only seventy, but the polio she'd had as a kid seemed to be revisiting her, and her body was giving out. I talked to her one Sunday and heard some hint in her voice that she was letting go. She went into the hospital Wednesday. On Thursday the nurse said, "You better get out here if you want to see her alive again."

My three sisters and my brother and I all got to the hospital by midnight. Mom was in some sort of coma, unable to speak. But we thought she could probably hear us, so we talked to her through the night and held her hands and made sure she knew we were there supporting her. And we told her that it was okay if she was ready to die, that we could let her leave this world and go where she needed to go. And in the morning she did. She died, all of us surrounding her with our lives and our breath. And then there was just a body where our mother used to be, and we knew she had departed. And in her place we had this new mountain to climb, this new grief to bear. But somehow, maybe just by being her children, we were able to see the trail, the way, the light.

ONE LAST LITTLE SOMETHING TO PUT IN YOUR PACK

(5)

Hint: It's not dried apricots

joy

Embrace it when it comes to you, let it go when it's time to leave,
and never stop believing it will come your way again.
Let's call that the Simple Secret of Life.

JOY IS PURE, UNADULTERATED DELIGHT. Joy can fill your heart to the brim with a blissful sense of well-being. It comes from out of the blue sometimes, unannounced and unexpected, like a long-lost friend. And when that friend shows up for supper, you don't want to be reserved or restrained. You don't want to hold back your emotions when you're in the company of joy. You want to offer your wide smile, your shining eyes. You want to be able to freely express the song your soul is suddenly singing. When you're walking with joy, joy will make you feel like you're walking ten feet off the ground.

Joy wants you to GET GIDDY over the magnificence of this fragile world. Fearlessly fall in love with life. Fearlessly believe that life will love you back. Thrill in the fact that you're moving, walking, searching. Climbing. And, as you climb, thrill in the miracle you are, the miracle life is. Be amazed. Be humble. Be goofy. Be alive. Don't worry. If you're doing all these things, Joy will find you. Joy always finds the party.

No, it won't be easy.
Of course not.
But, boy, can it be joyous.

Maybe it gets harder to give in to joy as we get older. But that's because joy's perfect companion is innocence, and neither one of them holds any interest in car payments, forty-hour work weeks, or even tomorrow. Innocence is totally into the now, the moment. It thinks mud pies are a great idea. Innocence likes to CARPE EVERY DIEM — not that it knows that's what it's doing.

In·no·cence (ĭn´ə-səns) *n*. **1.** The soul that hate and fear have not yet discovered. **2.** The heart where joy knows no bounds, where laughter isn't colored with guilt or regret. **3.** Not knowing what you shouldn't have to know.

MAYBE THE FIRST TIME WE EVER EVEN NOTICE OUR INNOCENCE IS WHEN WE LOSE IT. Somewhere along the way something hurts us. Our smile is not returned. Our laughter is not encouraged. Somewhere along the way someone claims we're not good enough or bright enough.

So there we stand, melting Popsicle in hand, with our innocence so newly lost. I wish I could say that our lives come to a fork in the road, or a diverging path. I wish I could say that at that point in our lives we make a choice. We either follow the way of cynicism and disappointment, or the way of gratitude and joy. Joy in spite of the loss of innocence. BUT YOU KNOW IT'S NOT AS SIMPLE AS THAT.

This life doesn't come down to just one choice. There's no right path and no wrong path. But there are better ways to go, better roads to take. And there are choices to make, choices you make. And there is joy on every path, but you have to seek it. And there is joy on every mountain, but you'll never find it if you're standing still. And you certainly WON'T FIND IT BY HIDING BEHIND FEAR OR DENIAL OR REGRET.

JOY IS LIKE THE SUN. Out in the open. Step outside the fear and feel the joy. Throw off the shroud of denial and feel the joy. Let go of the regret and feel the joy.

JOY REVELS IN YOUR KNOWLEDGE, YOUR EXPERIENCES, YOUR LIFE; IN HOPE, IN PEACE. In spite of travails and setbacks and switchbacks. Joy understands what you've been through, what you're going through, and will never try to stop the process. And the truth is, sometimes it seems as if there are too many fates that are conspiring against us. Too many battles to fight – be it alcohol or drugs, cancer or car accidents, divorce or abuse – to even consider the concept of joy. Sometimes it seems there's too much heartache for there to possibly be any joy left in this life.

But joy is patient,

and you are resilient. And that means, no matter how broken you might feel, it's always just a matter of time before joy taps you on your shoulder. Oh! And joy loves to sneak up and surprise you, a good surprise, with balloons and fruit punch and crepe paper. And mixed nuts, always mixed nuts. Joy appreciates the irony in mixed nuts. Mixed nuts atop the mountain.

Joy wants to see you smile at all the everyday graces that flow your way. Joy thinks being captivated by the most minor of miracles is a true art, a talent worth honing. Finding a new bird's nest in your backyard. Biting into a fresh-out-of-the-oven oatmeal cookie (with nuts, of course). These simple kinds of pleasures can bring you closer to FINDING THE JOY IN LIFE, in everything alive.

As a matter of fact, joy would like to call to your attention a miracle you may not have noticed, something truly amazing:

You have gotten all the way to page 139. THAT MEANS YOU CAN READ! And that means you can do something that more than one billion people on this planet can't do. (Go ahead, look it up.) At this very instant, your eyes are effortlessly focusing on the letters of our alphabet arranged in millions of different ways to form countless words. And those words are strung together to create sentences and ideas and thoughts. And the whole fantastic chain of events is completely second nature to you! The fact that you've got neurons firing inside your brain and that your brain is processing – at warp speed – all the information you are taking in is nothing short of awesome.

And that's not all. Do you realize that the fact you can read means you are one of the fortunate few who were lucky enough to land in a place where someone had the means and the drive and the know-how to want to help you learn? Someone decided that you were important enough for them to spend a piece of their time teaching you how to read in the first place. For that, my friend, there's only one word: WOW!

WHEN YOU HAVE JOY,

grati

tude

always follows. And gratitude brings humility. And humility brings awe and wonder. And that awe and that wonder give us hope for now, for tomorrow. And we know all about what hope brings... Yup, it's a beautiful circle.

Embracing joy is our simple secret of life, and joy is everywhere. You don't need a caravan of camels traveling across the Sahara to find it. It isn't buried in some bottomless tomb in the remote reaches of Madagascar – though it is priceless, and sometimes it seems so hard to find. IT'S A GIFT, joy is, and sometimes gifts are few and far between.

And, just between us, that's okay; that makes you love the gift even more. When joy shows up, grab hold of the moment. Let it interrupt, let it barge in, believe it when it says you look gorgeous. Dance with it. Let it remind you of what you're living for, of the joy in life. For there is joy in life. In your life. ON YOUR MOUNTAINS.

joy says, NO SINGS:
"I LOVE TO GO A-WANDERING ACROSS THE MOUNTAIN TRACKS AND AS I GO I LOVE TO SING…VAL-DE-REE! VAL-DE-RAA!"

I've been battling depression for years. Right now I'm winning, but there have been times when I believed that my life would never be right again. And when I'm depressed, a tremendous sense of apathy kicks in and takes possession of my brain. I don't care about anything and it really doesn't matter that I don't care because…what's the point? In the past, when the darkness took over, I would retreat to my room and sleep. I slept a lot. I tried not to dream. I tried not to think. I would lie there and listen to the clock tick. I would lie there and almost wish I were dead. Except I didn't care enough either way to do anything about it.

These days I take a magic little blue pill. A blue pill for my particular blues. And it's working. It's been working for three whole years now. I know that one day my brain chemistry might outwit the medicine and the depression will start creeping back. But one day isn't now. And right now I feel strong and clearheaded and optimistic. Clearheaded enough to know that the powerful truth is this: Even when I was lying in bed, drenched in sweat, without the will to try and pull myself together, I was climbing. Just by taking it day by day, I was climbing the invisible mountain in my brain.

WE WILL
DANCE ATOP THE
MOUNTAIN

6

Well, so here we are, almost to the end of this little book. You've made great time, don't you think? I bet you've covered ten miles since morning. There are some clouds to the east, but they don't look like they'll catch up with you – and, no worry, you've got a water-proof tent. Judging from the size of that backpack, it looks like you're prepared for just about anything. And prepared is a good thing to be when there are SO MANY POSSIBILITIES, so many choices, so many forks in the road. In just a few more pages, you and I are going to take separate paths. But before this leg of the hike is over, there's one more thing that I hope you'll always remember:

You have more control than you think you do.

The way you act and react to everything that comes your way is continually deciding how your story is going to be told. When you pack that waterproof tent, those extra matches and that triple dose of hope, you're off-setting a myriad of major and minor catastrophes.

surv

ivor

When you choose to see yourself as a born survivor and you try to handle all of life's crazy circumstances accordingly, you will be amazed at what you can withstand, what you can take, what you can bear. You can't pick the headaches and heartaches that come your way, but you can have a say in how you deal with them. Sometimes you can make lemonade out of lemons, order out of chaos...and molehills out of mountains.

So maybe you can't put a positive spin on everything, but you can try to make having a positive attitude be a way of life. Maybe you can't stop a mudslide, but you can be prepared to handle a little mud. (What do you think a bandana's for?) Life is what you make it. Life is how you shape it. And the more you fully invest yourself in every day, the more alive you become. With every challenge that rolls your way, you become more human, more valid, more real, more you. And only you can truly appreciate the depth and breadth of all the miles you have walked on earth. Your singular miles, your personal experiences, your custom-made mountains. And with that, I do believe you've got EVERYTHING YOU NEED.

AND SO...
Tally Ho!

Isn't it funny how the things you do need to take on your journey

HOPE
LOVE
STRENGTH
TENDERNESS
FAITH
JOY

they don't weigh you down.

AS LIGHT AS AIR, that's what they are. They make you light on your feet, light of heart. They put light in your life. And they don't, they won't, they can't hold you back. They won't put blinders over your eyes. They want you to be aware, to observe, to know all about the bad stuff, the hard times, the difficult decisions. And, as if by magic, these things you need to carry with you on this lifelong hike will fit nicely in your backpack, each and every one of them, with plenty of room to spare. With room to grow.

And isn't it funny how the things you don't need to take on your journey

TOUGHNESS
REGRET
DENIAL
FEAR

they do weigh you down like stones. That's what they are. On your back, in your shoe, on the road in front of you. They tear at you, they wear you out. They bend your spine, your resolve, your path. They're pathological. Manipulators. Liars.

But you know what you need to carry with you and what you need to leave behind. Yes you do. You know you need to travel light. After all,

YOU'RE A JOURNEYER, A SURVIVOR, A STILL ALIVER.

Maybe even more aliver than you were way back when, before. Maybe that person you were, the one who avoided those mountains for fear of whatever, feels like a stranger now. I hope so.

I have hope.
I hope you have hope.

There's still a long way to go. There's always a long way to go. But we all know it's the going and not the getting there that gives meaning to our matter, that makes us who we are. That's the crust on this sourdough loaf called life. And so with your pack packed, with knowledge in your head, with hope in your heart...I wish you well. I wish you well with gusto, with zest. With pride. And, if I might add (with a little drum-roll please): YOU'RE DOING A GREAT JOB! You're taking life and living right down the middle of it! (By the way, that's what it says on the sign at the top of your next mountain.)

Ahhh, your next mountain...

Oh, and life is such
a mountain, a miracle,
a bowl of cherries.

Climb!